HEROES AND HEROINES OF THE AMERICAN REVOLUTION

Brave Black Patriots

IDELLA BODIE

SANDLAPPER PUBLISHING CO., INC.
ORANGEBURG, SOUTH CAROLINA

Copyright © 2002 Idella Bodie

All rights reserved.

First Edition

Published by Sandlapper Publishing Co., Inc.
 Orangeburg, SC 29115

HEROES AND HEROINES OF THE AMERICAN REVOLUTION Series

Manufactured in the United States of America

Library of Congress Cataloging-in-Publication Data

Acknowledgements

I am indebted to Burke Davis
and other historians whose diligence in research
brought to light the proud legacy of black
Americans in the Revolutionary War.

To The Young Reader

American colonists issued a Declaration of Independence on July 4, 1776, which stated that all men had the right to be free. Yet slaves were not free. Many colonists did not own slaves nor believe in the practice of slavery, but they could not stop it.

When General George Washington took command of the Continental Army, blacks were not allowed to join. The freezing, starving experience changed that. Many whites left the army and soldiers were needed. Because the British were offering freedom to blacks who served on their side, the Continental Army began to welcome them. In fact, Rhode Island had an all-black regiment, which won honors for bravery.

It seems blacks could hardly be expected to fight for a country that kept them in slavery. Yet 5,000 slaves, as well as free blacks, served bravely on the side of the Patriots. Blacks were among the Minutemen in the first military skirmish of the Revolution at Concord, Massachusetts. They made contributions in every major battle, including Yorktown.

Even though the Continental Army accepted blacks into the ranks, some states did not. In South Carolina and Georgia, few blacks were allowed to "bear arms," that is, carry guns. Since blacks outnumbered whites in these states, the citizens feared armed slaves might rise up against their masters. There were, however, slaves in some of the southern militias, which were made up of volunteers. Francis Marion, the Swamp Fox, had blacks in his brigade. They fought with him in South Carolina in the battles of Cowpens and King's Mountain.

In all colonies, slaves and freedmen, blacks who had never been slaves or had bought their freedom, played a big part. They built forts, dug trenches, and made other preparations for battle. Fort Moultrie, on Sullivans Island, South Carolina, was erected almost entirely by slave labor. Blacks served as engineers, sailors, boat pilots, messengers, spies, and blacksmiths who marched with the soldiers to repair wagons and artillery. They were also orderlies who looked after their masters' personal needs and tried to protect them. Others were drummers and powder boys. Many served as combat soldiers.

Some masters sent their slaves into war to take their places. Others allowed slaves to go to war, and the masters received their pay.

As the struggle for the nation's freedom grew, more and more blacks became involved in the fight to secure their personal freedom from slavery. Freedmen had begun to organize a movement to gain freedom for all blacks in America.

Though blacks fought alongside whites during the Revolution, only a small number appear in historical records. Perhaps this is because laws in most states did not allow slaves to learn to read and write. On the other hand, many whites wrote letters home or they kept diaries. These personal writings have been passed down in families. White officers made reports and wrote memoirs. Yet few entered the names of blacks and their contributions. This book holds accounts of some black Americans whose deeds of bravery were recorded.

Contents

Crispus Attucks . . . *Martyr*	1
James Armistead . . . *Spy*	16
James Forten . . . *Powder Boy*	24
Austin Dabney . . . *Artilleryman*	31
Prince Whipple . . . *Bodyguard*	35
Peter Salem . . . *Minuteman*	41
Salem Poor . . . *Brave Soldier*	44
Agrippa Hull . . . *Orderly*	47
Edward Hector . . . *Wagoner*	53
Oliver Cromwell . . . *Oldest Veteran*	57
Antigua . . . *Carolina Spy*	59
George Latchom . . . *Savior*	60
MAP	62
WORDS NEEDED FOR UNDERSTANDING	64
THINGS TO DO OR TALK ABOUT	72
BIBLIOGRAPHY	76

Crispus Attucks
Martyr

1.
Runaway Slave

The first martyr in the fight between the colonies and their mother country, England, was Crispus Attucks. He is called a martyr because he was willing to give his life for freedom.

Little is known of Attucks's early life, but it is believed he was the son of an African father and a Natick or Nantucket Indian mother.

As an adult, Attucks was a slave. Though he was under the rule of a master, he had an independent spirit. People knew him as a ropemaker and a clever trader of horses.

More than anything Attucks wanted to be free. Unable to buy his freedom, he ran away.

No information is written about Crispus Attucks until 1750, when an advertisement appeared in the *Boston Gazette* newspaper. His master, William Brown of Framingham, Massachussets, placed the following notice.

MISSING PROPERTY:
A runaway slave. Six feet, two inches tall. About 27 years old. Wearing new buckskin breeches, blue yarn stockings, checked woolen shirt, and light-colored bearskin coat. Whoever shall return him, shall receive ten pounds. All are cautioned against concealing said slave under the penalty of law.

Attucks disappeared completely. It was believed he had become a sailor, working on a whaling crew out of Boston Harbor.

2.
Runaway Returns

Twenty years later Attucks was back in Boston, living not far from Boston Commons. He worked as a ropemaker for ships in the harbor. It is likely, since so much time had passed, no one even gave a thought that this ropemaker might be William Brown's runaway slave.

Colonists were angry about the taxes they were forced to pay to England. King George sent regiments of British soldiers to protect the men who collected taxes. The presence of Redcoats, the name given British soldiers because of their red coats, made matters worse.

The soldiers did not like being in America. The people of Boston would not let them rent rooms in their homes, and they were forced to live in tents in the public park. The tents were cold, and straw for beds was scarce. Town merchants would not sell them food so they had to depend on what British ships brought from England. Bread was stale, and other foods had mold or bugs.

Both sides, American and British, said hateful things to each other.

When skirmishes began in the streets, the British set a curfew. They ordered colonists to stay inside their homes after dark. The Americans paid no attention to this order. Even young boys gathered in the streets and threw trash at the soldiers on guard duty.

3.
Protesters Gather

On the evening of March, 5, 1770, a heavy snow covered Boston's icy streets, gardens, roofs, and woodpiles. Rumbling oxcarts and carriages packed the snow into deep ruts. The air was clear and still, the moon bright enough to see faces.

Protesters, black and white, gathered along King Street. Their footprints marked the snow. Their breath turned white with frost. They built bonfires and stood around them jeering at soldiers on guard at Boston Commons. Many protesters pelted Redcoats with snowballs, some with rocks in the center.

A Redcoat shouted at the rowdy colonists, "Go home, rebels!"

A young boy yelled a taunt at the soldier.

"Shut up!" the soldier shrieked.

The boy cursed. The soldier jabbed him on the head with the butt of his musket. The boy ran down the street yelling and holding his bleeding head.

Redcoats crawled from their tents and ran to the soldier's aid.

One of the colonists dashed to Old Brick Meeting House, where the Quakers held their church services, and clanged the fire alarm.

Soon streets filled with excited, frightened people. Thinking they were answering a fire bell, some carried buckets. Others carried swords, axes, pitchforks, and even boards ripped from buildings to beat back the Redcoats.

The crowd grew larger and pressed closer. Shouts and curses flew back and forth. Somebody in the mob yelled, "Lobsterbackers!" Being called a lobster because their coats were red like a lobster's back really angered the British.

More soldiers rushed from the tents. Pointing bayonets at the crowd, they moved the Americans back. The situation was turning into a skirmish.

4.
Out of Control

From the north end of town a group of American sailors, slaves, and workers from the loading docks hurried to join in. They were angry because off-duty British soldiers had taken many of the jobs on the docks, leaving them without a way to make a living.

The mob rushed up King Street. Leading the way was a giant of a man, Crispus Attucks. He urged his followers on in a booming voice. Over his head he waved a long, sturdy stick of firewood he had grabbed along the way.

The crowd divided to let the men through.

Attucks's great swaying stride took him within two feet of the line of Redcoats. "They dare not fire!" he yelled. "We're not afraid of them!"

Redcoats loaded muskets, brought them up to their chests, and aimed. Fingers touched triggers.

Attucks stepped forward, towering over the soldiers and swinging the stick of wood in the air above their heads.

"Stand your ground!" Attucks called to the colonists.

More snowballs hailed on the Redcoats. Clubs and sticks swung through the air with force. A swift blow knocked a soldier's weapon to the snow.

Attucks pushed closer and let out a blood-freezing war whoop. This time he faced a line of bayonets. With one hand he grabbed a bayonet. With the other he clubbed a soldier.

No doubt the anger that had built up throughout Attucks's life took over. Because he was born a slave, he could not own property. He was forced to live in poor quarters and he made only pennies for wages. All his life he had longed for freedom.

Redcoats panicked. Acting without orders, they opened fire. Muskets roared. Attucks fell to the ground. He lay dying with two musket balls lodged in his chest.

When smoke from gunfire cleared, five Americans lay bleeding in the snow, dead or dying from British fire.

News of the massacre spread. Crispus Attucks, a black man, was the first to be killed in what would become America's Revolutionary

War. This 1770 skirmish became known as the Boston Massacre.

Caskets of the dead, black and white, were brought to King Street for the funeral procession. All bells in Boston tolled. Shops closed. It is written that 10,000 people, from all walks of life, walked or rode in carriages in the funeral procession. Honored as heroes who shed their blood for liberty, the dead were laid to rest in Old Granary Burying Ground.

AMERICANS!
BEAR IN REMEMBRANCE
The **HORRID MASSACRE!**
Perpetrated in King-street, Boston,
New-England,
On the Evening of March the Fifth, 1770.
When FIVE of your fellow countrymen,
GRAY, MAVERICK, CALDWELL, ATTUCKS,
and CARR,
Lay wallowing in their Gore!
Being *basely*, and most *inhumanly*
MURDERED!
And SIX others badly WOUNDED!
By a Party of the XXIXth Regiment,
Under the command of Capt. Tho. Preston.
REMEMBER!
That Two of the MURDERERS
Were convicted of MANSLAUGHTER!
By a Jury, of whom I shall say
NOTHING,
Branded in the hand!
And *dismissed*,
The others were ACQUITTED,
And their Captain PENSIONED!
Also,
BEAR IN REMEMBRANCE
That on the 22d Day of February, 1770
The infamous
EBENEZER RICHARDSON, Informer,
And tool to Ministerial hirelings,
Most *barbarously*
MURDERED
CHRISTOPHER SEIDER,
An innocent youth!
Of which crime he was found guilty
By his Country
On Friday April 20th, 1770;
But remained *Unsentenced*
On Saturday the 22d Day of February, 1772.
When the GRAND INQUEST
For Suffolk county,
Were informed, at request,
By the Judges of the Superior Court,
That EBENEZER RICHARDSON'S *Case*
Then lay before his MAJESTY.
Therefore said *Richardson*
This day, MARCH FIFTH! 1772,
Remains UNHANGED!!!
Let THESE things be told to Posterity!
And handed down
From Generation to Generation,
'Till Time shall be no more!
Forever may AMERICA be preserved,
From weak and wicked monarchs,
Tyrannical Ministers,
Abandoned Governors,
Their Underlings and Hirelings!
And may the
Machinations of artful, *designing* wretches,
Who would ENSLAVE THIS People,
Come to an end,
Let their NAMES and MEMORIES
Be buried in eternal oblivion,
And the PRESS,
For a *SCOURGE* to Tyrannical Rulers,
Remain FREE.

5.
A Hero Remembered

Since war had not been declared, the soldiers who fired the deadly shots were jailed and tried for murder. John Adams, who later became the second president of the United States, defended the soldiers. He tried to make the jury see Attucks as a rabble-rouser, or troublemaker, rather than a person who loved freedom. Only two Redcoats were found guilty. Their punishment was to be branded on the hand and released.

Today, some groups still think of Attucks as a rabble-rousing villain. Others praise him as a patriot and martyr.

In 1858 historian William C. Nell and others started a Crispus Attucks Day. Citizens of Boston used that day to honor those who died in the fight for freedom. In later years this day of celebration was replaced by the Fourth of July.

In 1888 the city of Boston erected a statue of Attucks and a monument in Boston Commons to honor him and others who died in the massacre.

Many places and organizations bear Attucks's name. Pennsylvania has a Crispus Attucks Association. Virginia's Crispus Attucks Cultural Center, Inc., is raising funds to renovate the historic Attucks Theatre built in 1919. Indianapolis has Crispus Attucks Middle School. The name continues to be synonymous with courage.

James Armistead
Spy

1.
Slave Volunteer

James Armistead is remembered as one of the most important spies of the American Revolution. James's last name was that of his owner, William Armistead, a farmer near Williamsburg, Virginia.

In 1781, when Armistead was about twenty-one, he heard that the Marquis de Lafayette, a young Patriot volunteer from France, needed someone to spy on the British. James asked his master if he could offer his services to General

Lafayette at Yorktown. William Armistead agreed.

General Lafayette soon discovered that James Armistead was brave and smart. He was just the person needed to serve as an intelligence agent.

The British were offering freedom to slaves who joined their side. Layfayette asked Armistead to go to British General Cornwallis's camp and pretend he wanted to join their army. In that way he could find out secret information for the Patriots.

When Armistead appeared at the British camp and offered to be a servant and guide in exchange for his freedom at the end of the war, no one suspected he was a spy. Instead, they saw a smiling black man willing to serve their meals and guide them on roads unknown to them.

Armistead probably stood near General Cornwallis during meals. While he served food and drink, he listened. Often he aided Cornwallis in his tent. He always kept his ears open for talk about the war.

After gathering information, he secretly passed along what he heard to Patriot scouts waiting out of sight outside the camp. Even at the risk of his life, his reports went out almost daily.

2.
A Double Agent

General Cornwallis was impressed with Armistead's hard work and attitude. He was so convinced of Armistead's loyalty, he asked him to spy on the Patriots for the British army.

Now Armistead had the perfect setup. He could move back and forth between the two camps, carrying true information to the Patriots and bringing back false information to the British.

Cornwallis was a smart general, and he was careful to keep his maps and papers hidden. Still, Armistead was able to learn that British troops planned to move toward Virginia. He carried this information to Lafayette, who prepared his troops to follow.

Staying a safe distance behind, Patriots trailed the British through Virginia and to the coast from the Blue Ridge Mountains.

James Armistead knew being discovered as a spy could mean death. Yet, he continued to take messages from one camp to another.

3.
Surrender

One of the most important messages Armistead delivered was carried to the Patriots while Cornwallis's army was camped at Portsmouth on Chesapeake Bay. The report revealed Cornwallis's plan to unload his troops at Yorktown.

Based on Armistead's report, General Lafayette moved his troops there. General Washington sent word that French and American forces would join Lafayette to cut off British troops by land and sea.

Led by Lafayette's small force, Patriots surprised the British by surrounding them in the village of Yorktown. Ten days later, Cornwallis surrendered.

Standing in Layfayette's headquarters, Cornwallis saw the familiar face of James Armistead. His trusted spy was wearing an American uniform. Cornwallis grimly shook his head. He could not believe he had been fooled.

James Armistead played a crucial part in winning the final battle of the Revolution.

4.
After the War

Because of Armistead's admiration for Lafayette, he asked the general if he might take his last name. Lafayette replied that he

> **BE IT REMEMBERED!**
>
> **T H A T** on the 17th of October, 1781, Lieutenant-General Earl CORNWALLIS, with above Five thouſand Britiſh Troops, ſurrendered themſelves Priſoners of War to his Excellency Gen. GEORGE WASHINGTON, Commander in Chief of the allied Forces of France and America.
>
> **LAUS DEO!**

would be honored. From that time on, the former slave was known as James Armistead Lafayette.

General Lafayette praised the work of his spy. About three years after the war's end, Armistead sent Lafayette's written certificate of praise to the General Assembly of Virginia. He asked that, based on his war record, he be declared a free man. He added that he could only accept an award of freedom if the Assembly agreed to pay his master for the loss of his slave. The Assembly consented.

Although James Armistead Lafayette was recognized as a veteran who fought for his country, he was still not considered a citizen. He did, however, receive a military pension when he was in his sixties.

In 1824 the Marquis de Layfayette returned to America for a visit. He made arrangements for artist John B. Martin to paint a portrait of his faithful spy. In that painting James Armistead Layfayette, proud and dignified, wears a white neckcloth under a blue military coat. The buttons on his coat are embossed with an American eagle, the symbol of freedom.

James Forten
Powder Boy

1.
Love of Ships

Although James Forten's father came to America as a slave, James was born free in Philadelphia on September 2, 1766. As a boy James liked going to the Delaware River docks where his father worked on ships' sails.

James attended a Quaker school for blacks. Each day after school, he hurried to the docks where his father and other workers climbed tall masts to mend sails. He enjoyed watching the sailing ships maneuver to the docks to unload their cargo.

When James was seven, his father fell to his death from one of those sails.

In spite of his father's tragedy, James still loved the sailing ships. He quit school at the age of fourteen and signed up to serve as a powder boy aboard the *Royal Louis*. The ship was owned by a privateer who had

permission from the colonists to fire on and take goods from British vessels. It was James's job to carry gunpowder to the men firing on enemy ships. He also served as a drummer and beat the drums to summon sailors to work.

2.
Prisoner

Toward the end of the Revolutionary War the *Royal Louis* was captured by the British. Everyone on board was taken prisoner. The British captain headed to the West Indies to sell the black prisoners to plantation owners as field hands.

During the sail, James met the captain's son, who was the same age. The English boy liked the quick-witted American who played a fine game of marbles. The two became friends. James's friend begged his father not to sell James. The captain gave in to his son's wishes, even saying James could return with them to England.

"No," James replied. "I'm a prisoner for my country. I will not be a traitor."

Rather than leaving James in the West Indies with the other black prisoners, the captain took him to a British prison ship off Long Island. The captain thought he was doing what was best for James, but that was not the way it turned out.

3.
Hard Times

Aboard the prison ship James was shoved into the ship's smelly hold, deep below deck.

Along with thousands of other prisoners, he was forced to live on wormy meat, crust of moldy bread, and stinking water. Many prisoners died and were buried in the sand dunes along the ocean.

Once, James had a chance to escape. A Patriot officer held captive onboard was being exchanged for a British prisoner at a nearby American camp. James had made plans to hide in the officer's trunk. At the last minute he let a young white boy take his place.

After seven long months in the smelly cargo area of the prison ship, James finally convinced his captors he was born free in America. They let him go.

4.
Successful Businessman

Back home in Philadelphia, James Forten became an apprentice to a sailmaker. He was proud to follow in his father's footsteps. By the time he was in his thirties, he owned the company.

Forten invented a device to help crews handle heavy sails on large ships. A patent on his invention made him wealthy.

He fell in love with Charlotte Vandine, a slave. He bought her freedom and they married. The couple had five children.

The Fortens organized a group that worked to make slavery illegal. Forten wrote and published papers against the practice. He used his wealth to help poor, struggling black Americans. The Forten home in Philadelphia was located at 92 Lombard Street. It served as part of the Underground Railroad, helping black slaves escape to Canada.

James Forten lived to see his children and grandchildren become leaders against slavery.

He never regretted the years he spent as a drummer, a powder boy, or a prisoner for his country during the Revolutionary War. He died March 4, 1842.

Austin Dabney
Artilleryman

1.
Wounded

A slave owner who did not want to serve as soldier in the Revolutionary War could send a slave in his place. Austin Dabney's master sent him. Dabney was one of the few blacks in the South allowed to man heavy guns. Most southern blacks were not allowed to bear arms of any kind.

As a member of an artillery in a Georgia Corps, Dabney fought

under Colonel Elijah Clark. He fought in the battle of Cowpens in South Carolina. There, the Patriots killed, wounded, or captured almost all of the British and Tory soldiers.

Dabney was said to be the only black soldier at the battle of Kettle Creek. When he was seriously wounded with a rifle ball to his hip, a white soldier, Giles Harris, took him to his nearby farmhouse. He saw to it that Dabney was nursed back to health.

2.
Faithful Companion

Dabney never forgot Harris's kindness. Freed by his master after the war, he went to work for Harris. When Harris's son William was ready for college, Dabney went along to look after him. He often entertained William and his classmates with stories of the struggles between Patriots and Tories.

After graduation, Dabney worked to support William while he continued his studies in law. When William passed the bar exam, required to practice law, Dabney wept with joy.

3.
Honored

Although it was years before his courage in the war was recognized, Dabney was finally awarded for his heroism. In 1821 the Georgia legislature gave him a one-hundred-twelve-acre farm.

Dabney formed friendships with wealthy neighboring planters. He became owner of many fine horses. Being a landowner helped him receive a pension for his military service.

It is believed he is buried in the Harris Family Cemetery.

In 1977 the Pulaski (Georgia) Chapter of the Daughters of the American Revolution included Austin Dabney on a monument in Griffin Memorial Park.

Prince Whipple
Bodyguard

1.
Sold as a Slave

Until Prince Whipple was ten years old, he lived in the African village of Amabou. He was from a wealthy family and may truly have been an African prince as he claimed. His father sent him, along with a cousin, to America to be educated. An older brother had already received his education in the colonies.

The greedy captain of the ship on which the cousins sailed sold both boys into slavery near

Baltimore, Maryland. William Whipple from Portsmouth, New Hampshire, bought young Prince.

Prince lived in the slave quarters on the grounds of the Moffatt mansion. The home and grounds had been inherited from the Moffatts, the family of William Whipple's wife.

2.
Loyal Guard

When the Revolutionary War began, William Whipple joined up as a captain and an aide to General George Washington. He took with him tall, gentlemanly Prince to serve as his bodyguard. Prince was also a soldier.

On one occasion, Whipple, who was by then a

general, sent Prince to deliver a large sum of money to another city. When robbers attacked the young man, he beat off one with a heavy whip and shot the other. His master's money was saved.

3.
Soldier

Many black soldiers fought in the 1776 battle of Trenton, New Jersey. It is believed that Prince was the first to step ashore after crossing the Delaware River on that freezing Christmas night. He was surely near George Washington in 1776 as the Patriots marched through sleet and snow to Trenton to surprise Hessians who were busy celebrating the holiday. One thousand Hessians, hired to fight by the British, were taken prisoners.

4.
Free Again

Prince was promised his freedom after the war. But it was not granted until he and other blacks who were born free in Africa joined together to confront the New Hampshire legislature.

Once freed, Prince married Dinah, also a free black. The couple and their children lived in a two-story house near the Moffatt mansion. The house still stands today.

Prince was sometimes called a jack-of-all

trades, meaning he could do just about anything. An early historian recorded that Prince was loved by all who knew him. He was often invited to be master of ceremonies, the person who welcomes guests and sometimes gives a speech at formal events.

Prince Whipple died in his early thirties, leaving his widow and several children.

5.
Remembered

On July 4, 1908, one hundred twenty-five years after the Revolutionary War, veterans from Portsmouth, New Hampshire, dedicated a marker in North Cemetery to Prince Whipple.

The famous painting of "Washington Crossing the Delaware" by Emanuel Leutze shows only one black man. One report says it is Billy Lee, General George Washington's aide. Many believe it is Prince Whipple.

Peter Salem
Minuteman

Paul Revere and other Patriots galloped through the Massachusetts countryside warning, "The British Are Coming!" Peter Salem was one of the Minutemen who answered the call.

Born a slave in Framingham, Massachusetts, Salem was freed by his owner so that he could sign up with the Patriot army.

Several months after he fought in the battle of Concord, he was among the soldiers fighting at Bunker Hill. Salem became a hero in this battle when he shot and killed British Major John Pitcairn. The officer had ordered the Patriots to

retreat, but Salem refused. Instead, he loaded his musket again and again.

The musket he used in battle is displayed at the Bunker Hill Monument in Massachusetts.

It is reported that white soldiers proudly presented Salem to General George Washington as the man who killed the British officer at Bunker Hill.

Salem also fought in the battles of Saratoga and Stony Point.

After the war Peter Salem settled in Leicester, Massachusetts, where he barely earned a living weaving cane seats for chairs. He died in 1816 in the Framingham poorhouse. Almost seventy years later, the town erected a monument in his memory.

Salem Poor
Gallant Soldier

Little is known about Salem Poor's early life. He was born free in Massachusetts. He married young and lived on a farm with his wife. Like other colonists, he listened to the talk of breaking away from England. He decided he was in favor of independence.

When the Revolutionary War began at Lexington and Concord, Poor joined the Patriot forces. Like Peter Salem, he had a steady hand and eye. He too killed a British officer, Lieutenant Colonel James Abercrombie, at the seige of Charleston, Massachusetts, in the battle of Bunker

Hill. The Patriots held their position at Bunker Hill until they gave out of ammunition.

Patriot officers praised Salem Poor, writing to the Massachusetts General Court that "Poor behaved like an experienced soldier in his gallant and brave action as he fought in Captain Ames Fry's regiment." In spite of this petition, it is not

known if the Court rewarded Poor.

Poor remained in the army for many years. He fought in the battle of White Plains, New York, and lived through the bitter winter at Valley Forge.

In 1975, Salem Poor's image appeared on a United States commemorative postage stamp.

Agrippa Hull
Orderly

1.
Soldier

Agrippa Hull was born free in 1759. At the age of six, his family moved from Northhampton to Stockbridge, Massachusetts.

At eighteen, Hull enlisted as a private in the Continental Army to fight in the Revolutionary War. He served for six years and two months. Most of that time he spent as an orderly to George Washington's chief engineer, General Thaddeus Kosciuszko (Koz-chews-co). It was

Hull's duty to look after Kosciuszko's personal needs, such as food and clothing, and stay close beside him in battle.

2.
Friend to All

General Koscuiszko was not an American but a young Polish nobleman. He admired Americans for their brave struggle for freedom, and he came to help in the fight.

Since most American officers brought their personal servants to war with them, General Gates assigned Hull to Koscuiszko.

Hull was a man of great dignity, pride, intelligence, and humor. His quick understanding of situations and his performance of duties made him a favorite of all the officers.

3.
Battles

Hull followed Koscuiszko into the bloody battles at Saratoga in upstate New York and Eutaw Springs, South Carolina. He did not leave the army until July

1783, almost two years after the battle of Yorktown.

Hull and Koscuiszko formed a friendship. At the end of the war, Koscuiszko invited "Grippy" to return with him to Poland. Hull expressed appreciation for his friend's kindness, but he chose not to leave his homeland.

4.
Back Home

When Hull returned to Stockbridge, he worked as a butler until he made enough money to buy a farm. With a place of his own, he then married Jane Darby, a runaway slave. A young lawyer helped Hull gain his wife's freedom.

In his seventies Hull asked that his army pension be mailed to his home. He was told he must send his discharge papers to show proof of military service before the money could be sent. Hull replied that he would send the papers only with the promise they be returned.

"General George Washington signed my papers," he told those in charge. "Keeping his signature means more to me than getting the pension."

Hull died in 1848. He was almost eighty-nine years old.

5.
Memories of a Hero

"As long as Agrippa lived," one of the officers wrote in his memoir, "the children and grandchildren of friends from the war would visit him. They loved to hear him tell stories of the Revolutionary War."

Koscuiszko also visited his old friend on a return trip to America.

A portrait of Agrippa Hull hangs in the public library at Stockbridge, Massachusetts.

Edward Hector
Wagoner

It was Edward Hector's job during the American Revolution to drive and protect the ammunition and supply wagons. He always did his best to bring supplies and the horses unharmed through every battle.

In the September 11, 1777, battle of Brandywine, Pennsylvania, Hector fought bravely

lost, he was faithful to his duty.

During the battle, the order was given to abandon post. A few soldiers began to run, and then hundreds fled in fear. Into the mad rush for life Hector shouted, "Never! I'll save my horses or die myself."

Ignoring the struggle around him, he gathered up muskets left on the battlefield. Through what seems a miracle, he and his horses escaped injury. He saved wagonloads of ammunition and guns.

In the small town of Conshohocker (called Consky by its residents), located northwest of Philadelphia, is a street named Hector. It honors Edward Hector's act of bravery in the American Revolution.

Oliver Cromwell
Oldest Veteran

Oliver Cromwell was one of the last living soldiers of the Revolutionary War. He had fought throughout the entire conflict.

Burke Davis, in his *Black Heroes of the American Revolution*, tells of a spring day a reporter stopped at Cromwell's small house on East Union Street in Burlington, New Jersey. The reporter wrote that a thin, white-haired man, whose hands trembled with age, showed him his military discharge papers signed by General George Washington in June of 1783. The last battle of the Revolution had been fought seventy-one years earlier. The papers revealed that Cromwell had won the Badge of Merit for long, faithful service. This Badge of Merit, started by George Washington, is now called the Purple Heart.

Although Cromwell was one hundred years old, his memory, especially of the war, was still clear. He had enlisted as a private in the Second New Jersey regiment commanded by a very fat Colonel Shreve, he told the reporter. He remembered crossing the Delaware River in the attack on Trenton. His last battle was at Yorktown.

Oliver Cromwell died January 1853. He left behind children, grandchildren, and great-grandchildren, but no one marked his grave.

Antigua
Carolina Spy

A Carolina slave known only as Antigua risked his life to get information behind enemy lines. It is recorded that in March 1783 the South Carolina General Assembly praised Antigua for carrying out his military duties. In reward, they freed his wife Hager and their child. Although Antigua remained a slave all his life, the freeing of his family meant they could never be sold and taken from him.

George Latchom
Savior

Near the end of the Revolution, British soldiers landed on a shore near Yorktown. The only Patriots nearby, a small band of Virginians under Colonel John Cropper, fired on the British who were heading toward them.

The colonel moved out in front, leading the way for his men. George Latchom, a slave of Cropper's neighbor, moved with him. The rest of the troop held back.

When the British closed in with bayonets, Cropper and Latchom withdrew through marshy land. Suddenly the colonel sank to his waist in mud.

A Redcoat raced toward the colonel with his bayonet drawn. Latchom shot and killed the British soldier. Then he tugged the colonel to safety, even though the officer weighed over two hundred pounds.

Colonel Cropper bought Latchom from his neighbor and set him free.

It is written that Cropper felt he could never do enough for Latchom for saving his life. The two remained good friends until Latchom's death.

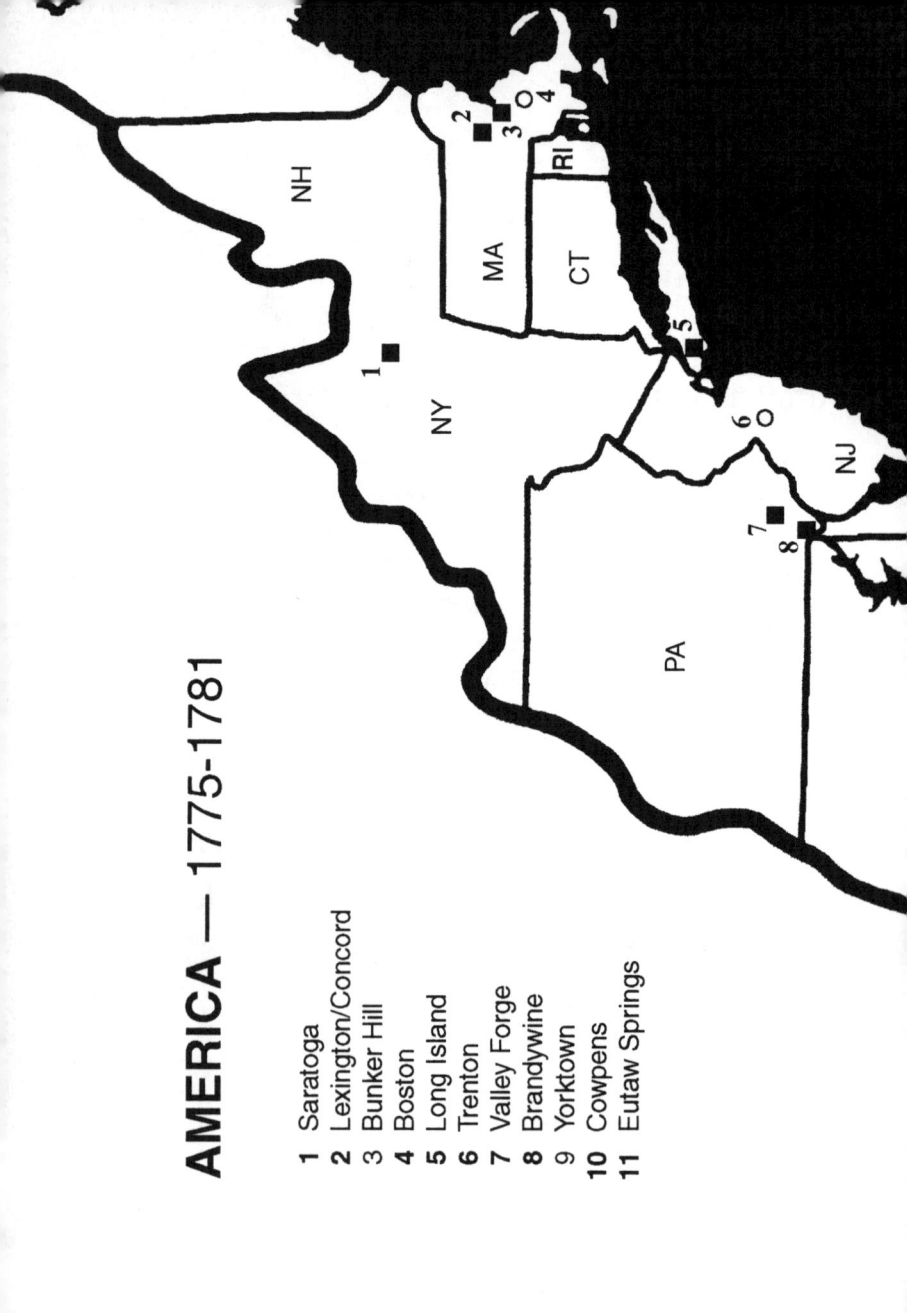

WORDS FOR UNDERSTANDING

abandon	leave a person or thing behind
ammunition	military supplies, such as musket balls
apprentice	a person who works under the guidance of another to learn a trade
artillery	large guns and cannons; a military troop that uses large guns and cannons
artilleryman	a person who belongs to an artillery unit; a person who uses large guns and cannons
band	a group of persons; in this case, a group of soldiers
bayonet	a knifelike blade attached to the muzzle of a rifle
bear arms	carry a gun

blacksmith	a person who makes objects, like horseshoes, out of melted iron and steel
bonfires	large, open-air public fires
branded	marked the skin with a hot iron
breeches	pants reaching to the knees
brigade	a large military unit
cargo	goods carried by ship
characteristic	a trait or quality that distinguishes a person
clever	quick in thinking
commemorative	showing praise, honor
consented	gave permission
corps	a special branch of the military
crucial	very important

curfew	a time after which people must remain indoors
daring	to act without fear
discharge	(as in discharge papers) indicating dismissal from service
engineer	one who designs military works, like forts
enlisted	joined
field hands	people who tend crops on a farm
gallant	brave and honorable
hold	cargo area on a ship
independent	free; not influenced by others in one's ideas and actions
invention	the creation of something that did not already exist
jeered	made fun of

maneuver	to make a series of planned movements
martyr	a person who suffers or dies for his beliefs
massacre	the ruthless killing of a large number of people
memoir	a written account of one's memories and observations
mend	repair
militia	a military company of volunteers
Minutemen	volunteers who could be ready to go to battle at a minute's notice
mob	a large, disorderly group of people, sometimes violent
musket	a long-barreled firearm
nobleman	a man born into aristocracy

orderly	a man assigned to perform personal services for an officer
panicked	became suddenly fearful
patent	legal ownership of an invention
pelted	threw fast and in large numbers
pension	payment made to a person who has fulfilled his military service
poorhouse	at one time, a group home for people who had no money; paid for by the government
powder boy	a young boy responsible for getting ammunition to those firing guns
privateer	the owner of a private armed ship authorized to attack and rob enemy vessels

protesters	persons, usually organized in a group, expressing disapproval of something, like England's tax law
Quakers	a society of Christians who teach peace and oppose war. Quakers are known for their simple lifestyle, family values, and hard work.
quick-witted	quick to understand
rabble-rouser	a person who tries to stir up anger in others
regiment	a military unit
rowdy	displaying noisy, rough behavior
savior	one who saves the life of another
scout	a person sent to gather information about the enemy

skirmish	a fight between small groups of troops
slave	a person who is property of another and obligated to work for him
stockings	heavy, long socks
stride	a person's way of walking
symbol	one thing that stands for another, like an eagle standing for freedom
taunt	something said to make fun of another person
tavern	a building where alcohol is sold to be drunk there; also, an inn, where travelers could sleep and get meals
tolled	rang slowly and repeatedly
Tory	a colonist who remained loyal to King George and fought with the British

traitor	one who helps the enemy
Underground Railroad	a network of people offering safe passage and hiding places to help slaves escape to the northern colonies and Canada
veteran	a person who has served in the military
villain	a bad person
wagoner	a person who drives a supply wagon
war whoop	a loud shout or call going into a fight

THINGS TO DO AND THINK ABOUT

1. In the Natick language "attuck" was the word for "deer." Do you know the meaning of your name? Would you like to find out?

2. At the time of the Revolution, the colonists used British pounds and shillings for their money. Can you find out how an English pound compares to a United States dollar today?

3. No one knows who actually started the deadly fight on Boston Commons, known as the Boston Massacre. Do you think both sides are to blame? Support your reasoning.

4. If Attucks was born "around" 1723 and ran away in 1750, can you figure how old he probably was when he escaped? If he stayed in hiding for twenty years, how old do you think he was when he was killed?

5. James Armistead carried messages about Benedict Arnold, the Patriot who turned traitor. Would you like to find out when and where this happened?

6. It is said that during the surrender of Yorktown the British played the tune "The World Turned Upside

Down." What do you think that title means?

7. We usually think of heroes as older persons. However, James Forten showed characteristics of a hero at an early age. What were they?

8. What is there about Forten's life that shows a person's future has a great deal to do with his attitude?

9. Hero Austin Dabney served under Colonel Elijah Clark. If you live in South Carolina or Georgia, you may be interested in finding out more about this officer.

10. If you live near or visit Portsmouth, New Hampshire, you may want to go to the site where Prince Whipple lived. You can see the slave quarters of his early years, which are on the grounds of the Moffatt House in the downtown historic district. The house where Whipple lived with his family in freedom is also nearby.

11. Records say Peter Salem died in the poorhouse. Do you think he was treated fairly? Why or why not?

12. A postage stamp was issued in honor of Salem Poor in 1975. Would you be interested in finding out who

makes the decision to do that?

13. Agrippa Hull was one of the free blacks who enlisted during the war. Why do you think he had so many friends among the soldiers?

14. I have said in Agrippa Hull's writeup that he was free when he enlisted in the Patriot army. Only one of my sources said Hull was not free until he was presented as a gift to General Thaddeus Koscuiszko. He was, this source said, immediately freed by the general and it was Hull's choice to stay. It is not unusual for sources to differ, especially about happenings over two hundred years ago. If you enjoy research, you can enter any hero's name in a Web search and find out more. Looking at the source given can help you determine if the information is accurate.

15. How do you feel about Edward Hector risking his life to save ammunition and horses? Do you think this shows a characteristic of a hero? Explain your opinion.

16. Oliver Cromwell valued the signature of George Washington on his discharge papers. Do you have signatures or autographs of persons you admire? You might like to share with your class how you got them

and why you wanted them? You could write up the experience and then share it.

17. Did you know that the battle of Bunker Hill was actually fought on Breed's Hill in Charleston, Massachusetts? The two hills overlook Boston Harbor. Try to locate them on a map.

18. Two artists are famous for depicting George Washington's crossing of the icy Delaware River. Would you like to research and compare the work of Thomas Sully who grew up in South Carolina and that of Emanuel Leutze?

19. Choose five of the heroes in this book you most admire and write a brief paragraph about why each is considered a hero. Include a main character trait you admire in each.

20. If you could talk to any hero in this book, which one would you choose? What would you ask him?

SOURCES USED

Billington, Ray Allen. "James Forten: Forgotten Abolitionist." *Negro History Bulletin,* vol.13 (1949): 31.

Bennett, Jr., Lerone. *Before the Mayflower: A History of Black America.* New York: Penguin, 1982.

Clarke, Corinda. *The American Revolution 1775-83: A British View.* New York: McGraw Hill, 1969.

Davis, Burke. *Black Heroes of the American Revolution.* San Diego: Harcourt Brace Jovanovich, 1976.

Fisher, Leonard Everett. *Picture Book of the Revolutionary War Heroes.* Harrisburg, PA: Stackpole Books, 1970.

Hamilton, Virginia. *Many Thousands Gone: African Americans From Slavery to Freedom.* New York: Alfred A. Knopf, 1993.

Ingraham, Leonard W. *An Album of the American Revolution.* New York: Franklin Watts, Inc., 1971.

Internet: Library of Congress: www.loc.gov
- *The Black American Almanac*, 7th ed., Gale Research, 1997.
- Independence Hall Association: "Negro Private in 3rd PA artillery," 2001.
- "James Armistead." Netscape: CIA Kids Page, *History,* December 16, 1998.

Internet:Public Broadcasting System: www.pbs.org/wgbh/aia ("Africans in America" series)

Millender, Dharathala. *Black Leaders of Colonial Patriots*. Indianapolis: Bobbs-Merill, 1965.

Nell, William C. *The Colored Patriots of the American Revolution.* Boston: Robert F. Wallcut, 1855.

Quarles, Benjamin. *The Negro in the American Revolution.* Chapel Hill, NC: University of North Carolina Press, 1961.

Smith, Robert. *The Infamous Boston Massacre.* New York: The Macmillan Company, 1969.

ABOUT THE AUTHOR

Idella Bodie was born in Ridge Spring, South Carolina. She received her degree in English from Columbia College and taught high school English and creative writing for thirty-one years.

Ms. Bodie's first book was published in 1971, and she has been writing books for young readers ever since. This is her nineteenth book.

Ms. Bodie lives in Aiken with her husband Jim. In her spare time, she enjoys reading, gardening, and traveling.

"Heroes and Heroines of the American Revolution" Series

The Man Who Loved the Flag
The Secret Message
The Revolutionary Swamp Fox
The Fighting Gamecock
Spunky Revolutionary War Heroine
The Courageous Patriot
Quaker Commander

Other Books by Idella Bodie:

Carolina Girl: A Writer's Beginning
Ghost in the Capitol
Ghost Tales for Retelling
A Hunt for Life's Extras: The Story of Archibald Rutledge
The Mystery of Edisto Island
The Mystery of the Pirate's Treasure
The Secret of Telfair Inn
South Carolina Women
Stranded!
Trouble at Star Fort
Whopper